Twirl for God

14 Day DEVO & Coloring Pages

Placing God at the center of your twirl world

By Michelle D. Howe

Foreword by Aubrey Howe

Color Illustrations by Doodles by Carlyn

Cover Photo by Athletes in Focus

All scripture quotations, unless otherwise noted are taken from YouVersion app from Life.Church using the New Living Translation.

To Morgan:

Thank you for shining your light and representing God in all you do. Your identity is solid in Christ and nothing will shake you. We are grateful for your example, encouragement and support to our family as we venture through this journey. We love you and pray for complete healing.

Table of Contents

Foreword

Introduction

Foreword

The first time I saw baton twirling was when I visited my cousin at a competition. I had no idea how long these competitions went on for so to pass the time I ended up with a baton in my hand learning some basic tricks.

Soon after, I tried out for the middle school team and was the only 6th grader that made the intermediate team mostly because I could do "fishtales." Yeah, I knew how to do those before I knew how to confidently do a "one-turn."

When I entered 7th grade, I decided I wanted to compete so I joined the local twirl team.

Six twirl seasons later, I have experienced many ups and downs. From competitions to my high school team, it's all been challenging but rewarding too.

I'll be honest, I'm still growing and learning what it means to be a Christian, to twirl for God, and how God desires to work in me.

One of my biggest struggles is I feel as though I'm never enough. Personally, this past year has been tough. I feel as though all I do is fail. I try and try and what's comes out is failure or that is what the enemy would want me to believe. But, God tells me something different like "I am enough," I am loved," and "I am significant."

I feel blessed to be surrounded at home, church, and twirling with leaders that continue to point me to the truth of God. I'm grateful for a mom that has walked this path and shares her wisdom with me and others.

I know you are going to love this DEVO my mom wrote. She is such an encouragement to me and so many other women. She reminds me daily that God is more interested in my character over my wins therefore,

I commit daily to keep him first in all I do and know he will work it all out in his timing.

When you are finished reading the DEVO, can I encourage you to read at the end about "Our Mission." I hope you connect with us so we can encourage you, and learn more about Dysautonomia (a condition I deal with).

Twirling, life, work or school may never come easy to me but I'm confident that God continues to use me in my weakness (2 Cor 12:9). This is true for you too. You don't need to have it all together to enjoy the blessings of God and all he desires for you. Just keep him first and he will work all things together for good (Romans 8:28).

Aubrey

.

Introduction

Welcome to the 14 Day Twirl for God DEVO!
Whether you are going through on your own, with family or with your twirl team, I pray God does his mighty work in and through you.

Each day of the DEVO gives you a verse, words of encouragement and a way to apply it to your life. Then, you will have the opportunity to use a coloring page to pray and meditate further on the lesson. When you are finished coloring, take a picture and share it with #TwirlforGod.

Originally this devotional was published through email. You can still sign up for free at TwirlforGod.com and receive them daily in your inbox.

From time to time, I do receive emails back from twirlers as they are reading through the DEVO.

Here is one I received from Carrie:

Hi! I wanted to let you know that this devotional has been such a blessing; I reread the emails before every twirling practice, as they make such an impact! I had always thought of baton twirling as a secular thing and that there was no reason that God should be involved in my "twirling life." However, after reading your words I realized that God should be the very center of my twirling world if I ever want to achieve my goals!

My favorite day of the DEVO was the one in which you mentioned thanking God after every drop--up until then, I had been saying negative things in my head whenever I dropped my baton, and it was very destructive. Getting angry after a mistake destroys self-confidence.

I have also realized that although twirling is a great and rewarding sport, I should always remember that there's more to life than just twirling, such as spending time with family and letting friends know how important their encouragement is in my life!

Finally, last year in May I tried out for feature twirler at my school, and worked extremely hard only to have

my band director choose another girl due to her senior-
ity. This crushed me, as I love twirling and performing
and it's my dream to be feature twirler. I was so dis-
couraged and kept thinking that I just wasn't ever going
to be good enough for the position, but now I am gain-
ing confidence since your devotional taught me that I
am good enough in God's eyes. I'm trying out again in a
few months, and I'm looking towards God for all the
help I need! Thank you so much for this great oppor-
tunity to connect twirling with my faith in God.

WOW!! All I can say is Glory to God for all he is doing
and is going to do through this DEVO. It's truly an
honor to be an instrument of God's grace and love.

I look forward to hearing how God uses this DEVO in
your life too. Message us on Instagram @TwirlforGod
or join our Twirl for God community group on Facebook. Let's encourage each other and pray for one another as God gives us the platform of baton twirling to
bring him honor and glory.

Day 1 – Placing God First

"In everything you do, put God first, and he will direct you and crown your efforts with success."
Proverbs 3:6

What is success to you? Is it moving to the next level of twirling, making the majorette team, or winning a pageant like Ms. Majorette? Those are great goals but success to God looks like growing your character and becoming more like him – like his son Jesus.

Now along the way of you placing God first in your life and at the center of your twirl world, success could come in the way of you reaching your goals but that is not God's promise.

His promise is that he will direct your heart and mind when you seek after him first then all will be added to you. (Matthew 6:33)

So, you may be thinking how do I put God first in my life?

Well, you have taken the first step with this devotional to begin creating a habit of being in God's Word daily and meditating on it – meaning thinking about how it applies to your life. Next, I would like to give you suggestions to help you apply the DEVO to your life with a section I call "Princess Practice."

Believe it or not, you are already a princess in God's eyes – His Twirl Princess! He created you and loves you just the way you are. This section of each day's devo is for you to learn to apply the lesson to your twirl world and other areas of life so you can be crowned with God-sized success.

Princess Practice: One of the most important things you do before you begin twirl practice is to stretch. During your time of stretching, I want to encourage you to also be talking to God. It may seem weird at first but try it. Pray for the twirl season, for everyone to be safe during practice and for your coaches and team members. End your prayer by telling God thanks for how he has blessed and gifted you. God loves a grateful heart. This will only take a few minutes during your stretching time and it will set you up for success and blessings.

Day 2 – You are a Masterpiece

"For we are God's masterpiece. He has created us anew in Christ Jesus, so we can do the good things he planned for us long ago." Ephesians 2:10

When you are outside, do you ever take notice of God's creation? He created everything you see – the flowers, trees, the sky, birds, butterflies and more! He is a master creator and his most prized creation is YOU! Do you believe that?

In today's verse, it is written that we are God's masterpiece – his handiwork. On most days, you may not feel this way but it's true. Unfortunately, much of your time may be spent comparing yourself to others or saying unkind things to yourself. These thoughts become your truth about who you think you are.

Princess Practice: It's time to start believing you are who God says you are – a beautiful masterpiece. Grab a few note cards and write down all the following statements.

- I am a masterpiece!
- I am enough!
- I am worthy!
- I am beautiful!
- I am loved!
- I am accepted!

After you write these down on your note cards, place one in your twirl bag, one in your school bag and one by our bed. Read them throughout your day to remind yourself of who you are in Christ Jesus and to counteract the "negative stuff" running through your head.

Day 3 – Do Not Fear

"Don't be afraid, for I am with you. Don't be discouraged, for I am your God. I will strengthen you and help you. I will hold you up with my victorious right hand." Isaiah 41:10

Today's verse is my daughter's favorite in this season of her life. She's in her high school years and competing with teams and individually in baton twirling. She loves the sport of twirling and watches hours of it on YouTube.

Sometimes, though, she becomes discouraged about issues at school or at church, or when she can't quite achieve a baton trick she needs to accomplish for a routine. Also, fear tends to creep in when she wants to have others think well of her or when she is comparing herself to others.

This is a dangerous road to walk when you are more interested in gaining the approval of others over God. Thankfully you have a God that loves you no matter what. There is no need to try to impress or be someone you weren't meant to be.

I want you to take a moment right now and read today's verse again but instead of reading the word "you," read it with your name inserted. Write in your name below and read it out loud to yourself.

Don't be afraid, for I am with you _____.
Don't be discouraged, for I am _____ *God.*
I will strengthen _____ *and help*
_____. *I will hold* _____ *up*
with my victorious right hand.

How awesome is that! What a great reminder and tool for you to use as you approach anything that might take your eyes from God and cause you to feel fearful or discouraged.

Princess Practice: Our mission with twirl for God is for you to place God at the center of your twirl world. It's easy to forget when you are all caught up in practice and competition day, so here is an easy way to bring him front and center. Place a rhinestone cross on your costumes to signify you are twirling for God. My daughter places hers on the right side near the hip area. Why? Well, as you read in today's verse, it references the right hand of God. In the Old Testament, a reference to the right hand of God is a reference to Jesus – an extension of the Father. Therefore, when you go to hit the floor or field, you will have a small reminder to place God at the center of your performance.

If you would like to see how to place your rhinestone cross, visit our Instagram page @TwirlforGod. Also, once you have placed the cross on your costume, take a picture and post it with #TwirlforGod. We want to celebrate and pray for you.

Day 4 – Confidence in Him

"Blessed are those who trust in the Lord and have made the Lord their hope and confidence."

Jeremiah 17:7

When you hear the word "confidence," what first comes to mind? Most likely, your first thought is self-confidence. The world screams at us to have confidence in ourselves because that's our source of strength, but this is not the kind of confidence God talks about in his Word.

God-confidence is your faith – faith that you believe what God says about himself, his Son and you. In Hebrews 11:1 it says, "Faith is the confidence that what we hope for will actually happen; it gives us assurance about things we cannot see."

Your hope and confidence must come from God. Anything else in this world will disappoint, and that includes your friends, family and coaches.

We are all human and we will make mistakes, say things we don't mean, and do things we shouldn't do.

Therefore, it's important to make God and his promises your confidence and hope so that when those in your life let you down, you can extend grace. God modeled this kind of grace when he died on the cross for your sins and mine.

Princess Practice: I invite you to go on a God hunt. Today I want you to be open to seeing God in your day. There are certain things that happen daily that are unexplainable. You could call them coincidences but I call them "God winks." If you have never experienced God this way, pray and ask him to make himself evident to you. He will show up when you ask so be ready to feel love in a way you may have never felt before. These are experiences that build your faith and confidence. You want to collect these moments, build on them, and write them down so you can remember and share them with others.

See God in your day

Day 5 – Tune into WPAT

"Don't worry about anything; instead, pray about everything. Tell God what you need, and thank him for all he has done." Philippians 4:6

I love how simple today's verse is. Don't worry. Pray. Ask. Give thanks. Though it seems simple enough, applying it can sometimes be a little more difficult.

When you learn a new twirl trick or a new concept at school, it all takes practice, practice, practice. God isn't looking for perfection, but progress, just like your twirl coach. Wow, isn't that a relief?

Perfection is a dangerous road to travel. I remember my daughter trying a new trick and becoming frustrated with herself because she couldn't master the trick perfectly as she had seen others accomplish at twirl competitions and on YouTube videos. I told her it takes time and practice. Also, it helps to not overthink it but to stop, take a breath and ask God for help.

God does care about the things you care about, so talk to him and tell him what you need help with, whether it's school, twirling or whatever.

Princess Practice: During school, work or practice, if at any time you begin to feel worried or anxious about anything, tune into the Twirl for God radio station – **WPAT**. When you feel **Worried**, **Pray** and **Ask** God for help then tell him **Thanks** just like our verse suggests.

Ok there is no such radio station, but what an easy and simple way to remember how to deal with feelings of anxiousness, perfectionism, worry and fear. **Tune into WPAT!**

Remember progress is the goal not perfection!

Day 6 – Strength for Anything

"For I can do everything through Christ, who gives me strength." Philippians. 4:13

You are most likely familiar with our verse today. You've seen it used by many athletes but in context this verse is not about physical ability rather it's about the ability to be content in Christ through anything.

In the verse before this, Paul says, "I have learned to be content with whatever I have. I know how to live on almost nothing or with anything. I have learned the secret of living in every situation, whether it is with a full stomach or empty, with plenty or little for I can do everything through Christ, who gives me strength."

These verses remind me of the movie, "Facing the Giants" when the coach tells them, "And if we win, we praise him; and if we lose we praise him. Either way. We honor him with our actions and our attitudes."

This new team philosophy of "I'm satisfied no matter what" caused them to show up differently as individuals and as a team.

This is the kind of strength you will have in a surrendered life to Jesus. This strength allows you to be content or satisfied regardless of the situation because your strength, worth and identity isn't in the world, but in him.

If you don't have the prettiest strut costume, you are satisfied!

If you don't have the best spot in the group routine, you are satisfied!

If you don't have the twirl partner you desire, you are satisfied!

Again, God is more concerned with your character then your trophies. He wants you to be content in what you have and who he created you to be.

For you can do everything through Christ who gives you strength!

This kind of satisfaction doesn't come over night. Rather it grows when you spend time in God's Word and with his people.

Princess Practice: Spend time today evaluating your relationships. Ask yourself these questions:

- Are the people I'm hanging out with daily making me better or bitter?
- Are the people I'm reading about and watching online drawing me closer to God or away from him?
- Who are the five biggest influencers in my life? (consider online influences too)
- Who can I spend more time with to help me be who God desires for me to be? (a mentor, coach or teacher)

Let me encourage you to use the blank space below to write down your answers to these questions. Then, pray and ask God to direct you on how you can start living in his strength so you can say, "God is enough and I'm satisfied!"

Day 7 – It's Not All About You

"Don't be selfish; don't try to impress others. Be humble, thinking of others as better than yourselves. Don't look out only for your own interests, but take an interest in others, too." Philippians 2:3-4

I love the straight-forwardness of God's Word. I think it's funny that God must tell us not to be selfish because he knew we would be. Also, he says don't try to impress others because he knew our hearts are driven to the applause of man.

These sets of verses could be your daily prayer to set your heart and mind on God as you head to twirl practice, school or work.

You could pray, "Lord help me today not to be selfish. Help me to see the needs of others and be willing to offer encouragement and support."

Next time you are at practice, think of this verse as a quick prayer (remember during your stretching time) so you can open your eyes to those around you who could use a little boost of encouragement.

Here are some ideas:

Next time…

- When you see a team member struggling with a trick, go over and offer some help.
- When you see a team member coming off the floor in tears, go over and give her a hug.
- When you see a member from another team looking scared out of their mind for competition, go over, grab her hand and tell her she is going to do great.
- When you see your coach looking as though she is going to pull out her hair or go out of her mind, stop and say a prayer for her.

Truly this is what it means to Twirl for God. It's not just about you, but about others too.

Princess Practice: Talk to God and ask him to give you eyes to see the needs of those around you like the examples I gave. Also, take a moment to ask forgiveness from God for the times you were too self-focused and ask him to show you where in your life you could make some changes to be more concerned for others.

Let me remind you again that God isn't looking for perfection but progress.

I'm personally still working on being obedient to this verse. It doesn't come natural and God understands. He knew we would need to hear it repeatedly.

Day 8 – Shine Your Light

"God is within her, she will not fall; God will help her when morning dawns." Psalm 46:5

Today's verse is such a beautiful promise especially as you approach twirl season. As you know, competitions start early, before the sun rises. This verse is a great one to start your morning, as you prepare for a full day of competing.

In context, this verse is from the Old Testament and is referencing the Holy City of Jerusalem where God dwelt among his people.

Now in the New Testament in Matthew 5:14, Jesus says, "You are the light of the world, a city on a hill that can not be hidden."

As followers of Jesus, redeemed by his blood, you are this city on a hill – God's dwelling place. If you have confessed faith in Jesus as God's Son and believe that he rose from the grave (Romans 10:9), then he is talking about you.

The last part of these verses says, "Let your light shine before men in such a way that they may see your good works, and glorify your Father who is in heaven"

I just love this!!!

God is in you and he desires for you to be his dwelling place so your light can shine out in all that you do. Therefore, when you twirl, dance, march or spin, you are shining for Jesus – for his honor and glory.

Princess Practice: Take this verse and place your name where it says "her."

God is in the midst of _____; she will not fall. God will help _____ when morning dawns.

I would encourage you to write this verse down with your name inserted in the blanks on some note cards.

Then, place some in your competition bags (preferably your cosmetic bag) so as you are getting ready you can remember to shine your light. I promise this will infuse you with God-sized confidence, hope and peace.

14 Day DEVO

Day 9 – Humble Yourself

"Humble yourselves before the Lord, and he will lift you up." James 4:10

Twirl competitions are awesome! A full day of fun, right?

Ok maybe it's not all fun! The long days bring on bleacher butt, headaches from hearing marching music for many hours, and interesting attitudes from worn out parents and kids.

My first season as a twirl mom were not some of my best moments. My competitive spirit got the best of me and God convicted my heart. I spend time apologizing and clearing up misunderstandings. In other words, I choose to humble myself rather than being right.

This doesn't come easy, but when you spend time with God your highest goal is obedience to him. Out of obedience flows blessing! Trust in the promise of today's verse "Humble yourselves before the Lord, and he will lift you up."

Princess Practice: Has there been a moment recently or in the past that you maybe didn't say the nicest words to someone or didn't quite react the way you should have? I know we've all been there. It happens, and God desires for you to make it right. Today, I encourage you to write a note or speak to the person God is placing on your heart. Your goal is to clear off any wrongs done or any misunderstandings that have caused bitter feelings. This person could be your coach, parent, team member or teacher. You can simply start with telling them how much you appreciate them, then share how you want to make it right.

I know this is a very grown up and possibly an uncomfortable request, but that's good. When you feel butterflies in your belly, it means you are growing in your walk with God and taking risks for his glory and honor.

Way to go!

By the way, if you need some help going to talk to someone, ask your parent to help you. I bet they would be willing to help you to write a note or to call someone you may need to makes amends with.

I'm so proud of what you have achieved so far with this DEVO. Here you are, finishing day nine! If you have done most of the practices, you are certainly in the realm of having God at the center of your twirl world.

Congrats and keep it up!!!

Day 10 – Building Your Character

"We can rejoice, too, when we run into problems or trials, for we know that they help us develop endurance. And endurance develops strength of character, and character strengthens our confident hope of salvation. Romans 5:3-4

As I mentioned before, God is more interested in your character than He is about your individual and team wins. Your character grows as you learn to lean on God to help you overcome difficulties, thereby producing strength, patience and confidence.

Think of it this way: Imagine you are the baton and God is the baton twirler.

When God is twirling you around (the baton) you can achieve incredible feats just like the Elite twirlers around the world. Without God in your life twirling you around, you will fumble and fall, and life just won't flow quite right.

A new believer in Jesus is like a new twirler – not quite confident in what they are doing, but with practice and commitment, they will grow in skill. This is the same with your walk with God. As you practice being with him daily, you begin to gain confidence and grace.

Princess Practice: Next time you practice, think about this concept: You are the baton and God is the baton twirler. Visualize yourself placing your whole life into God's hands and trusting that he will not drop you.

Also, next time you go out and practice, use those moments you drop your baton to pause and give God thanks for loving you and keeping you in the safety of his loving arms.

You can say…

"God, thanks for continuing to build my character so I can be strong in you."

"God, thanks for holding my life in your hands and protecting me."

"God, thanks for the gift of baton twirling."

"God, thanks for all the people you have placed in my life to make me who I am today."

God loves a grateful heart, so use your baton drops to give him thanks rather than a negative attitude.

Oh by the way, don't try this during your actual twirl performance. Baton drops aren't welcome on those days!

Let me say here that it's exciting to see you start trusting God more each day. Keep it up, and keep practicing putting him at the center of your twirl world. I promise God has you. He will not drop you!

14 Day DEVO

Day 11 – Encourage Each Other

"So encourage each other to build each other up, just as you are already doing." 1 Thessalonians 5:11

As I sit to write this, my heart is heavy learning that a dear friend and one of the biggest encouragers in my life has passed away. I apologize to start this way, but I feel as though I need to share so that you know how important it is to be an encourager to others, and to have some encouragers in your life too. It's essential for you to tell those in your life how much they mean to you, because life is short.

In a competitive sport like baton twirling, we can be so caught up in the spirit of it that we forget that real people and feelings are involved. It's important to remember that everyone is God's child, and we want to treat them the way we want to be treated.

In God's Word, he says, "Build up and encourage one another" over seven times. In my mind, this isn't a nice suggestion but a command. Therefore, we want to be on mission as the Twirl for God community to encourage and build up those around us, not to tear them down.

Princess Practice: Write down in the space below three or more people you consider your biggest encouragers or cheerleaders. Now send them a text or write them a hand-written note telling them how much you love and appreciate them. This is so powerful and something I encourage you to do often. If you have a Facebook page, consider writing a note of thanks or encouragement on their profile page. Not only will they see it but all their friends will too. It will bless them, I promise!

Day 12 – God's Twirl Princess

"Whatever you do, work at it with all your heart, as though you were working for the Lord and not for people." Colossians 3:23

When you hear the word "work" does it make you think what you will do for a job when you grow up? That would seem to make sense but the word "work" in to-day's verse means "anything" you do for God.

You can be working for God as a student, an athlete, as a mom, a teacher or as a bagger at the grocery store. It doesn't matter, if your heart is set on honoring God.

Did you know that God has a reward for you for working for him? Yes, he has for you what is called the "Crown of Life" (James 1:12). It is a special reward for those that dedicate all their work to God. This crown is yours for the taking when you decide to live your life for him first and not to please your friends, parents or even your coaches.

Also, I'm thrilled to tell you that God is your banner (Exodus 17:15). Just like the banner the winners receive when they win their twirl pageants, God has a banner for you too. This banner is one that becomes your shield and protection from the enemy. Also, it serves as a reminder of God's love and faithfulness.

Don't be surprised when you decide to Twirl for God that darkness or sin will want to tempt you back! Therefore, it is important and essential for you to choose to put on these items each day – your crown (the work you do for God) and your banner (your shield and protection).

Princess Practice: Do you have a crown or banner sitting around your room from a past pageant win? If so, let it represent the "crown of life" from God to you representing your choice to work for him. Also, let the banner represent his love, protection and guidance in your life. If you don't have a crown or banner, ask a parent, coach or friend to help you make them. Check out the dollar store or craft store to find some fun tiaras or crowns. It doesn't have to be expensive. Also, you can make your banner with 2" ribbon from the craft store and use some craft or glitter paint to write the message "I Twirl for God" or "I Am God's Twirl Princess." Again, place these items in your room as a reminder that you are choosing to work for God and desire to do it with all your heart.

By the way, making these banners and crowns could be a fun team building activity with your twirl team. You never know how God may use that in someone's life. They may come to know Jesus as their Savior by sharing how they are God's prized possession (James 1:19).

Reminder: Share the images of your commitment to be "God's Twirl Princess" by posting on your social media using #TwirlforGod.

Day 13 – Leaps of Joy

"The Lord is my strength and my shield; my heart trusts in him, and he helps me. My heart leaps for joy, and with my song I praise him." Psalms 28:7

I just love this verse! It's such a great visual of a man who was so devoted to God. This man was King David, who is mentioned as "a man after God's own heart" (1 Samuel 13:14). He knew God so intimately and wrote such beautiful words of praise and worship in the book of Psalms.

In 2 Samuel 6:14, we find David so enthralled with God that he danced with all his might before the Lord leaping and jumping around with no care in the world for what others might think of him.

Can you imagine performing for God in this way – without a care in the world, freely expressing your love and appreciation for your God?

I believe this is a good goal to set – to perform with all your heart for the Lord, regardless of the drops, missteps, or judge's opinion. I truly believe that when you perform this way, God will bless you beyond what you can think or imagine (Ephesians 3:20).

Princess Practice: One of the ways I encourage my daughter to prepare for competition is to sit, close her eyes and watch herself performing her routines – catching her tricks, smiling and loving each moment. Next time you are chilling before a competition, sit with your eyes closed and imagine yourself performing for God. Like David, imagine yourself doing your very best for God and see him smiling over you. Now that's powerful!

Cailyn ♡

Day 14 – Deep Roots

"Keep your roots deep in him, build your lives on him, and become stronger in your faith, as you were taught. And be filled with thanksgiving."

Colossians 2:7

Today's verse will serve as your daily prescription as we close out this DEVO. This verse will empower you to keep God at the center of your twirl world. We have covered most of this during our time together but this verse brings it all together.

1. Create Deep Roots – A tree knows to develop roots down into the ground and attach itself to the source. Your root is to be secured to God, thereby continuing to grow deep as you spend time in his Word.

2. Build Your Life on Him – Just like twirling, when you learn a new trick and you keep building on it, you will eventually advance. This too happens when you walk daily with God continuing to build your faith and confidence.

3. Give Thanks – As I have mentioned before, God loves a grateful heart. Out of a content and satisfied heart flow blessings. Therefore, talk to God throughout your day and give him thanks even for the little things.

If you take what you have learned from this devotional and apply it your life, I promise God will bless you above and beyond what you could ever hope for or imagine. It may not look the way you think it should look, but he will bless you for your commitment and obedience to place him at the center of your life and at the center of your twirl world.

Conclusion

"Don't shine so others can see you, shine so that through you, others can see him." C.S. Lewis

Well you have finished this DEVO but God isn't finished with you. He will continue his work in and through you as you seek him daily.

I encourage you not to just toss this book to the side or place it on a shelf. Rather, put it in your twirl bag or a bag you use often so you can flip to a page from time to time to remind yourself of the lessons you've learned. Also, it's a great way to acknowledge how far you have come in your walk with God.

Lastly, share your color pages and what you have learned from this DEVO with your parent, coach, teacher or friend. Tell them how you have grown in the Lord, and what God showed you about placing him in the center of your life.

I'm so proud of you, and would love to celebrate with you. Take a moment and send me a message at michelle@everydaylifeline.com. Share with me your prayers, dreams and goals. It would be my honor to lift these up to the Lord. I'll be praying too that you continue to keep your eyes on God as you venture forward in life and twirling.

Many blessings,
Michelle

Our Mission

Twirl for God exists to encourage baton twirlers to perform for God first and lean into him for confidence and grace.

We want to be your encouragement to keep God at the center of your twirl world therefore we invite you to connect with us at TwirlforGod.com. Learn more about us, the ministry and read our monthly devotional. And while you are there, grab a Twirl for God shirt or decal to show your commitment and share the love of God with others.

Another mission we are passionate about is spreading the word about Dysautonomia. Aubrey was diagnosed with Neurocardiogenic Syncope – a form of Dysautonomia - in September 2016. She suffered from symptoms of dizziness, headaches, shortness of breath, heart palpitations, heat and exercise intolerance, low blood pressure, brain fog, pains in her extremities and extreme fatigue. This condition does not have a cure but is managed with changes in diet and sometimes medications. Today she is better with the knowledge of the condition and support of her coaches.

Learn more about Dysautonomia (dysfunctions of the autonomic nervous system) at thedysautonomiaproject.org.

A portion of each Twirl for God book will go to the Dysautonomia Project to help fund awareness and finding a cure.

Lastly, I invite you to visit my personal website at michelledhowe.com. Besides my blog and leadership coaching, I offer additional devotionals to rise up and build confidence, evidence and purpose.

Made in the USA
San Bernardino, CA
16 March 2018